Puppy Parenting In An Apartment

CASSIE LEIGH

Copyright © 2014 M.L. Humphrey

All rights reserved.

ISBN: 978-1-950902-54-5

Also published under ISBN 978-1507819555

TITLES BY CASSIE LEIGH

DOG-RELATED
Puppy Parenting Basics
Puppy Parenting in an Apartment
Dog Park Basics

DATING FOR WOMEN
Online Dating for Women: The Basics
Online Dating is Hell

DATING FOR MEN
Online Dating for Men: The Basics
Don't Be a Douchebag
You Have a Date, Don't F It Up
The How to Meet a Woman Collection

COOKING-RELATED
You Can't Eat the Pretty

CONTENTS

Introduction	1
The Advantages To Puppy Parenting In An Apartment	3
The Disadvantages To Puppy Parenting In An Apartment	7
The Type of Apartment You Live In Matters	11
Breed Matters	15
Naming Your Pup	21
What You're Going To Need For You	23
What You're Going To Need For The Pup	27
Establish A Routine	35
The Go Bag	37
What To Take To The Park	41
Letting Your Dog Loose	45
What To Take To The Dog Park	47
Dog Park Etiquette	49

Exercising Your Dog	53
Toys—General	55
Pulling Crap Out Of Your Pup's Mouth	57
Back To Toys—The Noise Issue	59
Puke And Poop	61
The Fights You Lose	63
Riding In The Car	65
Commands You Should Know	69
Feeding Your Dog Human Food	71
What To Do For A Sick Stomach	73
A Great Vet Is Worth Their Weight In Gold	75
Make Friends With Your Neighbors And Management	77
Dealing With Children	79
Conclusion	81

INTRODUCTION

August 2013 I became the unexpected but proud owner of an eighteen-pound, eleven-week-old Newfoundland puppy. She's one of the best things that ever happened to me, but it's also been quite an adjustment and lifestyle change.

Taking on a puppy is much like having a child suddenly thrust into your arms.

(All my friends with kids hate it when I compare puppy parenting to parenting a child. But there really are a lot of parallels between the two. Lost sleep. Inability to figure out what this crying little creature wants from you. Doing things like leaving your keys in the door all night. Handling disgusting things you never thought you'd touch. Caring about your "child's" puke or poop including when and what it looks like and…Yeah. Lots of similarities.)

It's not like I'd never had a dog before. I grew up with them. And we usually had three at any given time. But that was twenty years ago and we didn't live in an apartment, so the experience was unique for me in many ways.

This book is a quick guide to the lessons I learned along the way. Hopefully it helps others that find themselves with a puppy in an apartment and aren't quite sure what they've gotten themselves into.

THE ADVANTAGES TO PUPPY PARENTING IN AN APARTMENT

There are some distinct challenges to parenting a puppy while living in an apartment (see the next section), but there are also many advantages. For example:

1. Better ability to train the puppy on what to eat/not eat.

Puppies explore the world with their mouth. They have no idea what's good for them or bad for them, so they pretty much try everything. More than once.

If you live in an apartment, every time your puppy interacts with the outside world you'll be there with them. Which means you can train them not to eat all the lovely things they want to eat. Like pinecones, leaves, rocks, dead animals, rabbit poop, etc.

And, oh yes, I fished every single one of the things on the above list out of the pup's mouth at some point in time.

2. You'll be better able to monitor your pup's health.

About two weeks after I got the pup she ended up with giardia. Since I walked her every day and picked up her poop every single time, I immediately knew something was wrong and took her to the vet. If she'd been running around in the backyard doing her thing, it could've been a few more days before I noticed. And a sick puppy is not a good thing. They're little creatures with a lot less ability to handle colds and infections than adult dogs, so when something goes wrong it can turn serious fast.

3. You'll raise a more socialized dog.

I took the pup to training classes when she was about four months old. (With Newfies the earlier you can get them trained, the better.) The trainer said you should try to expose your dog to a hundred different people of all shapes and sizes by the time they're six months old. Same with strange dogs.

I laughed.

We were already far past that mark. Pup was cute as cute can be, which meant that people were always walking up to us when we were outside. We probably met a hundred people in the first two weeks I had her.

A socialized dog is better behaved and more adaptable to changing circumstances. Face it, most of us are going to move in the course of ten years, which means new people, new places, and new dogs. The more your pup is used to variety, the better they'll handle it.

4. You'll raise a more disciplined dog.

My mom has a dog that she raised in a home and only rarely takes anywhere—maybe Petsmart and the vet every few months, but otherwise the dog lives in her yard and house. Well, when he does go anywhere he strains against the leash and pants and acts the fool. (They've also found at their new home that he actually refuses to go for walks at all.)

Pup? We had to go for walks four or five times a day, if not more, when we lived in an apartment. She very quickly learned how to walk well, how to sit, and to wait calmly instead of straining at her leash. Granted, that initially required my hugging her to hold her back from chasing rabbits or sniffing other dogs, but she learned fast.

She had to. It was the only way to keep her safe and me sane on our walks.

5. It will make you more social.

I'm a recluse. I work from home and generally socialize with family and a few close friends and that's it. Before I had the pup, I'd drive up to the apartment building, immediately walk to my apartment, and stay there until I had to go somewhere. If I saw someone I'd smile, but I almost never talked to my neighbors.

After I got the pup? I think I met almost everyone in my building. And we had long, lengthy discussions. Either they had dogs of their own and our dogs had to sniff each other, or they thought the pup was so cute that they just had to come meet her. Add to that the people I met at the dog park and Petsmart and on walks in the park and…Yeah. The pup definitely expanded my social interactions. Mostly in a positive way.

(Again, we're talking about a cute and friendly puppy here. For the most part the people I talked to liked her, so they were nice to me. If she'd been unfriendly? Who knows.)

THE DISADVANTAGES TO PUPPY PARENTING IN AN APARTMENT

As much as I am grateful for the fact that I raised the pup in an apartment that first year, there are also some disadvantages to it, too.

1. You Are More Likely to Give In to Crying/Barking

My pup liked to sleep near me when she was young. (Now she shuns me, but that's another story…) She decided after a few months that she didn't like sleeping locked in my bedroom, so she'd cry until I let her out.

Then she decided that if she was going to sleep in the living room, so should I, and she'd cry until I came and slept on the couch.

Little sounds, thankfully, but still crying at two in the morning. I had two choices: Wait her out until she quit or just go sleep on the couch. I chose to sleep on the couch. One, because I wanted to get back to sleep, but, two, because I was sensitive to the fact that she could wake the neighbors and I'd end up with a noise complaint.

If I'd been in a house, I would've probably waited her out. But when you're in an apartment you do not want your neighbors to complain about your dog. That's a good way to end up moving or losing your pup. So you find yourself giving in on things a lot more than you probably would if you lived in a house.

2. You Are More Likely to Have Moments Where You Kind of Hate Your Puppy

I love my pup. I do. I have made life-changing decisions because of her. But…When it was four in the morning and ten below outside and I had to bundle up to take her out because she was crying and barking to get out and then we got outside and she peed quickly and decided it was the perfect time to lay down in the snow and not move, I came close to really not liking her.

We're in a house at the moment and the fact that she can go outside on her own without me makes both our lives easier. She gets to enjoy the outdoors, I get to do my thing and stay warm. Or cool, depending on the season.

You don't really have that luxury in an apartment. Every time the pup needs to go outside, so do you. It's a disruption to your routine, your meals, your television watching, and your sleep. (I don't think I managed to finish a single hot meal the first six months I had her.)

When they're little, ignoring those cries can easily result in someone peeing on the carpet. So you really have no choice but to respond to them. It's stressful.

She barks more now that we're in a house, but a lot of the frustrations I had in the apartment are now gone.

3. You Are More Likely to Hate People

For me, it was the smokers first. Because they throw their cigarette butts everywhere and the pup tried to eat every single one she found for about the first month.

Then it was the other dog owners that didn't have the class to pick up after their dogs. Step in someone else's crap once or twice and you really start to dislike people.

When I was in DC, it was the people who randomly discard chicken bones on the sidewalk. (I am not shitting you. It was the weirdest thing in the world how often we ran across discarded chicken bones.)

When you live in a house there will still be moments when you dislike people. (Like the ones that power walk five times a day by your house. Or the ones who walk their dog and let it stand on the other side of your fence staring at your dog while your dog is going nuts.)

But more so when you have to get out in the world five times a day and interact with folks and the weirdness they pull.

4. Your Pup May Get More Sick

They tell you to keep a new puppy away from other dogs for a while because its immune system just isn't ready to handle all the nastiness that other dogs might have.

Well, I can tell you that's a near impossibility in an apartment building. You can wave people away and try to body block anyone who comes near, but it's just not going to work. There will be people who have no control of their dog or who ignore you and let the dog come over for a sniff anyway.

Not to mention, your dog is sniffing the pee and poop of all those other dogs, so it's going to be exposed to all that stuff no matter what you do.

THE TYPE OF APARTMENT YOU LIVE IN MATTERS

I was very fortunate that I was living in the ideal apartment for puppy parenting at the time I took the pup on. (When I moved to DC I was not, but by then she was well-trained.)

What made it ideal?

1. I was on the ground floor.

First, this made it easier to get a puppy with a small puppy bladder outside and onto the grass in time to do her business. Second, she's a big breed puppy and prone to hip and knee dysplasia. They've done some studies that taking dogs like that up and down stairs when they're less than six months old can make them more prone to that kind of issue, so I was able to spare her that added risk.

I met some folks who lived in a high-rise apartment with their pups and they had much more difficulty training their pups to pee outside, because a little puppy can't hold it in long enough for you to get dressed, call the elevator, get on the elevator, make it through the lobby, and get outside.

And if you use those puppy pads, well, you've just trained your dog that it's okay to pee inside at least some times. Better than the elevator, but still. Not ideal.

2. It was in a quiet area with lots of grassy spaces for the pup.

I had plenty of choices when I walked the pup, and we were able to have a nice relaxing walk.

(Even then we had challenges. The pup would get distracted at any little thing. She'd be about to do her business and someone would call to her and she'd stop and it would take another ten minutes before she was ready to do it again.)

I had a friend who got a puppy while living in an apartment in New York City. I walked the dog with him one day and I have to say I felt so sorry for that beautiful dog. The dog literally did its business over a street grate in the middle of the street. That after navigating its way around tons of people and walking on crowded, concrete streets.

That's a huge stress to a little puppy. His dog handled it well because it was a good breed for city living, but it wasn't an ideal situation.

3. They allowed big dogs.

As I mentioned, pup is a Newfie. They're generally over a hundred pounds full-grown. Some get into the one-sixties or more.

Most apartments have a seventy-five-pound limit. (Although you can sometimes ask and get them to agree to waive the requirement, which is what happened when I moved to DC.) Some apartment buildings even have a twenty-five-pound limit. I was lucky that mine had no limit on size.

Ignore those limits at your own risk. Because if they choose to, they can evict you for violating them. Or force you to get rid of the dog, and that would just be cruel to take on a pup knowing it isn't allowed and then have the pup pay the price for your mistake.

4. They allowed her breed.

My apartment had a list of breeds that weren't allowed at all. Generally, lists like that include breeds known for barking a lot or being aggressive. It can be a surprising list, because it's not size-based, so you should definitely check those restrictions before you get a dog.

And, trust me, if you're living in an apartment you don't want one of those breeds there anyway. You have neighbors. And you will run into people *all the time*. I mean, *all the time*. It's hard enough to control a well-behaved, quiet dog in those situations. I wouldn't even want to try controlling an excitable breed that snarls at someone. That's a good way to have your lease terminated early.

(One of those times when having a child is easier than having a dog. If you have a crying baby that keeps the neighbors up at all hours no one's going to tell you to move or get rid of the child. Barking dog that wakes the neighbors in the middle of the night? You could find yourself on the street or having to give up the dog.)

🐾 🐾 🐾

So, to sum it up. What are some of the qualities for the "ideal" apartment:

1. On the ground floor, ideally with direct access to outside.
2. In a quiet area.
3. Plenty of grassy areas to walk the dog.
4. Allows dogs as big as that dog will be when full-grown.
5. Allows that breed of dog.

Also, dog friendly. It's not a requirement, but it makes life easier. When I was in Colorado the people in my complex loved dogs. They really did. When I moved to DC? Not so much.

It was hard on the pup to be around people who saw her as an annoyance. It broke her little heart. It also made it extremely challenging to navigate the lobby and elevator when there were people who either glared at the pup like she was scum on the bottom of their shoe or who would actually get out of the elevator when we got on because they were scared of or disliked dogs so much.

Far easier to raise a puppy with people who are sympathetic to the challenges of doing so.

And the apartment buildings that are pro-dog have nice amenities like dog runs (a lifesaver in snowy weather when you can't drive anywhere) and free poop bags and large, convenient areas for the dogs to use.

Now, obviously, we don't all have the ideal circumstances. Good news is that dogs are resilient as all get out. Whatever environment you put a dog in, it'll adapt. But if you can arrange for the above, you and the pup will have a much more pleasant puppy parenting experience.

Because, trust me on this, it is HARD to raise a puppy. Especially if you're new to this. (I cried a few times the first month.)

It's worth it (just like kids are), but there are challenges and sacrifices that you'll make to get there.

BREED MATTERS

If you're reading this book, you probably already have your puppy. But if you don't yet, then think long and hard about what breed you'll get and whether you'll get a rescue or not.

I was very, very fortunate. Newfies are eager to please, intelligent dogs. The pup has never—that's right, never—pooped in the house. When we were in DC she got some sort of stomach bug that gave her the runs. She literally woke me up, waited for me to get dressed, waited for the elevator, waited until we got outside and on the grass, and then got sick.

(She has puked inside many a time. Although she got to the point where she'd start to make those retching noises and let me find something to put in front of her and then puke into that. Once all I could find was an empty tissue box, but pup puked in it like a champ.)

She did pee inside a few times, but even there she was mostly trained to go outside within about a day. Once she realized that I expected her to go outside, she did. The only times she had accidents after that were when she had a urinary tract infection and when I didn't catch her signals that she needed to go out in time.

Not all breeds are as easy to house-train. Read up on any dog breed you're considering to see what the challenges are with that breed. Even now, if you already have the pup, you should read up. That's how I learned that Newfs need obedience training as soon as you can manage it.

Newfies are a quiet breed, too. When we lived in the apartment she would rarely, if ever, bark at people walking by outside or in the hallway. She wouldn't even bark if someone knocked on the door. Only things that set her off were loud, screaming kids running up and down the halls, the doorbell, and other dogs barking.

(The first day I had the pup I also had a major water leak from the unit above me. Pup sat there behind her puppy gate and watched the men coming in and out to tear up the carpet, set up a large drying fan, and replaster the wall without ever once uttering a sound. Not standard behavior for all breeds.)

Newfies are also a low-exercise breed. Not a no-exercise breed by any means, but lower than many. When I was in the apartment and working from home we usually did two half-hour to hour-long walks a day. When I was taking her into daycare each day (yes, she's spoiled), we'd do one long walk at the end of the day.

In contrast, I knew folks from the dog park who would run with their dog to the park, let them play for an hour, run home with them and the dog would still want to go back outside almost immediately. Me on the other hand? I drove the pup to the dog park, let her play for an hour, drove her home, and she slept for four hours.

So, find a breed that can handle the confinement of an apartment or you will end up (a) with a very destructive dog that drives you insane or (b) spending all your spare time exercising your dog.

Newfies are also a nice breed. I've never seen the pup snarl at a person or dog. There've been times she should have. She once had a small dog who just attached itself to her tail and wouldn't let go. Pup turned around and stared at it like she couldn't understand what the hell that annoying thing hanging off her tail was, but she didn't snap at it or growl.

I will say the more time she's spent at dog parks and in

daycare, the more she's learned to stand up for herself. She has a spin move she does now when dogs try to mount her, because she is not having that, thank you very much. But, still, no aggression.

Which isn't to say that we haven't had a few bad moments. She barks when scared, and one day someone came rushing out of a crowded elevator and she started barking at them and they freaked out and it was bad because she was about seventy pounds at that point and has a very deep bark. The girl's mother complained to management. (Fortunately, everyone who worked there seemed to love the pup, so they didn't make an issue of it with us.)

Your life will be easier if you have a dog with a mellow temperament that tends to be quiet and low energy. Because one thing you'll find is that a dog that doesn't get enough stimulation will take it out on your belongings. Or the apartment.

The higher energy the breed, the more you need to exercise and entertain them.

Now to the rescue issue. I am all for rescuing dogs. But if you're new to having a dog, there are some challenges with rescues. I don't have a rescue, obviously, but many of the people I met in my building or at the dog park did.

So, what were the challenges?

1. Attachment Issues

This comes in a couple of flavors.

One dog I knew would not let the dog walker walk him. He loved his owner, but anyone else scared him. So the dog walker would came mid-day to walk him and the dog would hide and refuse to leave the apartment.

Another I knew would not walk through the doors of Petsmart. He'd been taken there for adoption events and associated it with a negative experience.

That's a problem for a couple reasons. One, when pup was going insane but the weather was too hot or too cold for me to spend a long time outside, I'd sometimes take her to Petsmart or Petco or somewhere like that just to burn off some of that puppy energy. Two, that's who I used for daycare when I was in DC.

If I hadn't had the option of taking her there, I hope she would've been okay somewhere else, but many rescue dogs don't know how to play or socialize with other dogs, so they don't pass the testing at many of the daycares.

And if you have a rescue and you leave them alone for long hours, it may be more traumatic to them than it is to a normal dog. (Personally, if it's more than four hours, I take pup to daycare. I put myself in her shoes and can't imagine what it's like to be left alone with nothing to do for that long. We're talking about a creature that when I first had her couldn't fall asleep unless her paw was touching some part of me. To leave her alone for eight hours at a time just seems too hard, but I know that's what people have to do.)

2. Aggression Issues

We had a rescue when I was little. She'd been abused by a man in her previous home, so she tended not to trust men. Well, my grandpa came over and he threw me into the air as you do with babies, and the dog bit him. She was a great dog, but her background had trained her that men could be mean and abusive, so she tried to protect me.

I've seen rescues also have problems at the dog park for similar reasons. They don't know how to act, so they sometimes react poorly to other dogs or people. If you're in an apartment, this is a much bigger deal than if you live in a home.

In an apartment you *have* to interact with other people and dogs. You have no choice. In a house, you can control the environment and limit exposure to other people and dogs.

3. Poor Training

A rescue may be harder to train. They may chew more of your things or have more accidents. Since an apartment isn't yours, this can be a real problem.

Now, keep in mind, this isn't the dog's fault. None of it. It's like a child that was beaten. They have no control over that. So don't make it worse by yelling and taking out your anger on the dog. There may be times you want to, but you'll do much better if you can be calm and soothing and show them what you want instead of yelling at them for what they've done wrong.

(Of course, I say this as someone who has a breed that responds well to praise and treats. So, know the breed of dog you have and train them accordingly. I seem to recall there are certain breeds that require a much more firm approach.)

NAMING YOUR PUP

This isn't directly related to living in an apartment, but it does matter a lot more if you're in an apartment than a home.

Why? Because you will use that dog's name so many times and have to tell so many people what you've named it, that you better like the name you chose.

My pup was not originally mine. My mom bought her but couldn't keep her because she was attacked by my mom's other dog. Which means she already had a name when I got her.

My mom had named her Priscilla. As in, Priscilla Queen of the Desert. (My mom loves fancy names for dogs…)

I didn't like Priscilla, so I changed it to Miss Priss. (And she really is one at times, let me tell you.)

Well…

Try saying "Good job, Miss Priss" every single time your dog poops for three months. (An excellent approach for potty training.) And try telling every stranger you meet that your dog's name is Miss Priss. See how much you like the name then.

(That would be why pup gets called "kiddo" ninety-nine percent of the time now.)

So, choose wisely.

I read somewhere that you should give your dog a two-word or two-syllable name. Something fairly basic that won't get confused with other common words. Seems like a smart idea to me.

All I know is that you should choose a name for your dog that you can say with a straight face.

WHAT YOU'RE GOING TO NEED FOR YOU

There are eight million things you'll need to buy for your puppy. But there are also things you'll probably need to buy for yourself, too. Here are a few of them:

1. Vacuum Cleaner

You may already have one, but is it up to vacuuming up all that dog hair? If not, you'll need a new one. One with the attachment function that allows you to get into all the crooks and crevices and lets you vacuum your couch.

I also recommend buying a Swiffer Sweeper. Very handy for all the dog hair that accumulates in the corners of bathrooms, kitchens, and entryways.

(Again, know your breed. Some dogs shed fine hair year-round. Some blow out their coats a couple times a year. Know what you're getting into.)

2. Hand Lotion

Why hand lotion? Well, you may not do what I did, but I was constantly picking weird things out of the pup's mouth. Or off her coat. Which meant I washed my hands about ten times as much as before I had her.

My hands were dry and cracked perpetually for the first six months I owned her. Lotion was essential. (Although, fun fact about my pup, she loves lotion. So putting it on and keeping the pup from trying to lick it off was often an interesting experience.)

3. Better Outdoor Clothes

I lived in cold-weather environments with snow (Colorado and DC). I had coats and gloves and boots, so I was fine. Or so I thought. What I had were clothes that were good enough for walking from my apartment to my car and then from my car to my office. They were not good enough for standing in the middle of a snowy field for twenty minutes with a puppy who wanted to enjoy the snowstorm.

I had to upgrade all my winter gear.

Most of us have the luxury of choosing when to leave our homes. If it's too ugly, you postpone that trip to the store until later. With a puppy, you don't. You will walk that pup in rain, snow, hundred degree temperatures, and insane wind. Whatever weather is possible where you live, you will be out in it. So prepare.

4. Pajamas That You Can Wear Outdoors

I had some cute pajamas that went into the drawer and never came out again after I got the pup. Why? Because I figured out that when the pup woke me at two in the morning, my life was much easier if I could just get up and get her outside without having to change.

When it was winter-time, I'd sleep in those thermal leggings and then throw on the pair of sweats I'd left waiting by the door. Only took about a minute.

5. Sunscreen

Sometimes pup and I would be outside for half an hour or an hour. Sunscreen was essential.

(And, yes, there is someone reading this that thinks I'm too permissive with my puppy and that I should make her do her thing and drag her back inside as soon as possible. There was a guy like that in my apartment complex. The door opened, he walked the dog five feet to the grass, it did its thing, and he took it back inside. My question, though, is why treat a living creature like that? My dog loves to be outside. She loves to enjoy the sun and the snow and the rain and the whatever. Oh sure, I have my limits, but I can't see crushing her little spirit like that. To me it's about finding balance between making her happy and having my own life. No one forced me to take responsibility for her, so I try to do my best by her.)

6. A Lint Brush

Personally, I'm lucky not to need this with the pup. She seems to shed in little clumps and I rarely find her hair on my clothes, but when I was growing up, these definitely came in handy. Run it over yourself before you leave the house so your clothes aren't decorated with that extra layer of puppy hair.

WHAT YOU'RE GOING TO NEED FOR THE PUP

This is an insane list. I may not even do it justice, but we'll try.

1. A collar or harness and leash

You need something to walk your pup with.

There was one family in our complex who got this cute little boxer puppy. And they'd take it outside without a collar or leash all the time. Don't do that. I was walking the pup one day and the boxer puppy ran across the parking lot to say hi to her. One, that dog could've easily been hit. Two, because it wasn't collared and leashed, the kid who was walking it had no ability to control it or pull it away from the pup, which he needed to do because it was running around my legs and pup was running around my legs after it. Not fun.

So, find what works for you in terms of walking your dog. Understand, too, that your pup will grow and you need to make sure the collar or harness still fit as it grows. When the pup was young, I left her collar on her all the time. She needed to be walked too often to deal with putting it on her each time. But I also made sure to check it regularly to make sure I could still fit my fingers under the collar.

(I heard some horror story of a dog that went into the vet because its collar had melded into its flesh because the owners weren't checking that the dog had enough space available between its skin and collar. This was a well-loved dog, too.)

I'd also recommend a fixed-length leash. I have a six-foot one that works great. Those adjustable ones that wind onto a reel and can be expanded or not? A disaster every time I've seen them used. The owners that I've seen use them are rarely in control of their dogs and it's much, much easier for two dogs to get tangled in them and panic and hurt themselves.

2. Food and water bowls

If you have a larger breed dog, think about getting a raised feeder. It's better for them if they don't have to dip their heads to eat out of their food and water bowls. (Helps prevent bloat.)

Also, this is probably unique to Newfies, the pup used to love to spill her water bowl all over the kitchen floor and lay in it. Problem solved when I got her the raised feeder.

(I swear, Newfies go for any source of water anywhere. I've seen pup lay in a mud puddle and run up and down an irrigation ditch in a field…If it has water in it, she'll find it and be soooo happy to get wet it's almost comical.)

3. Blankets

When I was growing up we didn't do this, but I now have throw blankets on every couch. (I'll talk more about losing the couch fight later.) It makes keeping things clean easier. When pup was young, before she could get on the couches, it also gave her places to curl up and know were hers.

4. Dog Beds

I didn't have these right away, but eventually I got the pup dog beds to sleep on. She knows they're hers and is pretty good about sleeping on them, which keeps everything else that much more clean and manageable.

(For example, right now she's sleeping on the bed I have for her in the office. Well, mostly. She likes to hang her head off the edge, so she's about 90% sleeping on the bed.)

I cover each of her dog beds with a throw blanket so I can clean them easily. ($8 a pop at Big Lots. You can't go wrong with a bunch of throw blankets.) Also, she used to love to chew on the beds, so this keeps her from doing that, too.

Keep in mind that your dog may not like every dog bed. I bought the pup one that was kind of poofy. She never slept on it, but she did try to destroy it multiple times, so I had to take it away.

A lot of puppy parenting is trial and error and finding what works for your particular pup.

5. Food

Obvious enough. You have to feed your puppy.

Try to start with whatever they were eating before and, if you need to, slowly transition to something new over the course of about a week by mixing the two for a while. Also be consistent with what you feed them or else they'll have digestive issues. Bad enough in a house, a potential nightmare in an apartment.

Also, puppy food for puppies. The bigger the breed, the longer they need puppy food. Talk to your vet to get their recommendation, although I will say one vet told me to transition the pup anywhere from one to two-years-old, which wasn't particularly helpful.

Also know that you'll be adjusting how much your pup eats depending on what stage of growth it's in. There was a point where I fed the pup six cups of food a day. She was skinny as could be even with that much food. Now, at eighteen months, my vet wants her down to three cups a day. Keep an eye on their waist and belly to see if they're getting too fat. A fat pup is a pup with stressed joints and other potential health problems, no matter how cute it may be.

6. Treats

You'll very likely need treats for training your pup. Even if you eventually get your pet clicker-trained, it starts with treats. (You use the clicker and treat at the same time so that the pup associates the clicker sound with the pleasant experience of receiving a treat until finally you can just remove the treat and use the clicker and the pup has the same pleasant experience. Thank you, Pavlov.)

I tend to over-treat the pup. But life is easy because I do. She gets into the car without any problems because she gets a treat when she does. She walks out of Petsmart without an issue because I feed her treats to distract her from all the other dogs.

Of course, we're talking small treats here. And never enough to make her fat.

7. Toys

I'll have a couple sections later on toys, but you need toys. Puppies like to chew on things.

You can either give them puppy toys or they'll chew on your things instead. Your choice. Better, in my opinion, to give them toys.

Each time they chew on something they shouldn't, you take it away and give them their toy. They will eventually learn what they can and can't chew on.

It's also good for bonding with the pup. I avoided playing tug-of-war games with the pup, because I didn't want any sort of dominance issues between us, but that's more a personal call.

8. Protective gear

The first winter when it was bitterly cold, I tried to get the pup to wear those booties that protect a dog's feet. It was a miserable failure. But I have a friend with Chihuahuas who has sweaters for each one that they have to wear when she walks them in the winter because it's just too cold for them otherwise.

Know the breed, know what it can or cannot take. Some dogs need sunscreen in the summer months. Some need sweaters in the winter.

Some, like my pup, go swimming in the lake when it's just above freezing and don't seem to care.

9. Pet odor and stain remover

Even the best pup (and I think mine was one) will have an accident. They will pee or puke or poop in your apartment. It will happen.

Before we managed the "puke in this bowl" trick, the pup puked on the floor and couch. And a few times when I missed her signals to go out, she peed on the carpet.

You need a stain and odor remover to handle those situations. If you don't really get the pee out of the carpet, the pup will continue to pee in that spot because it will smell the ammonia from when it peed there before and think that's a good place for it to use. Don't let that happen.

(And if you suspect there are pee stains you can't see, I've heard a UV or black light can be used to find them.)

10. A puppy gate

You need a puppy gate so you can start the puppy in a small space in your apartment. Like the kitchen, for example. You can slowly expand their area as they learn that the whole apartment is their house, but if you don't start small you'll probably have more indoor accidents and other issues.

A puppy gate is also useful if you need to run somewhere and don't want the pup to have access to the full house with all its temptations and dangers.

I had a fantastic puppy gate that could stand on its own and was adjustable so I could move it to different rooms. For example, when I first had the pup and she slept in my room, I'd put the gate in my walk-in closet to block the pup from getting to all my shoes that were on the ground. During the day, I used it to keep her in the kitchen or entryway. As she got older, I made it bigger and gave her access to more space.

11. A crate

Now, I did not crate-train the pup. I wish I had. I had a crate, but she never took to it and I didn't force the issue.

I managed okay without one, because I figured out her schedule and knew that when she fell asleep she was out like a light for two hours, which gave me time to run to the store real quick. And she liked to sleep in the kitchen or bathroom, so I could put the gate in place and know she was contained. But having her crate-trained would've definitely made life easier for me. (Especially after she figured out that I left during her naps and started sleeping in front of the door.)

For folks that work all day and need to leave a pup at home, I think a crate is probably essential. Pups will rarely mess in their environment if it's a small, contained space.

(Of course, just because that's true doesn't mean you should push it. A puppy won't want to pee in its crate, but you leave it long enough and the pup's not going to have a choice. I once told the pup to wait a minute while I finished doing something and she tried, but she just didn't have it in her to hold it in any longer. She let out the most pathetic little cry and peed in the middle of the living room. It was clear she didn't want to, but she just couldn't wait any longer. Leave a pup in a crate too long and the same thing will happen.)

12. Benadryl

Your pup is out in the world. You will likely need Benadryl at some point for either an allergy or a bug bite or to help calm them on a long car trip or if they get scared at the vet.

Although I don't think I ran into the bite issue until we lived in a house. She found bees out in the yard and three times in four days managed to get herself stung by them. One time her ears both swelled up. One time she had a bite right under her eye that swelled to the size of a marble. And one time on her lip. After that first expensive ER visit when I worried her throat would swell shut, I just gave her a healthy dose of Benadryl instead.

Ask your vet for proper dosage/usage. For many dogs it can also be used to calm them down. Makes them a little drowsy. For others, it makes them more hyper, though, so know if that will work with your pup or not.

13. Puppy wipes

These came in very handy. Pup would get all sorts of dirty or smelly and I could just rub her down with a wipe rather than try to give her a full-blown bath. (She wasn't really one to roll in nasty smells until the day I took her to a friend's house and she discovered either cat or raccoon poop and dropped and rolled in it. Solution? Puppy wipes.)

14. Brushes and combs and all that.

Again, know your breed. Pup needs brushing on a regular basis. At least twice a week, but I usually try to do it more often because she seems to love dirt. She will happily lay in a mud puddle and not think a thing of walking around covered in dried dirt for the rest of the day.

Get your pup used to being groomed early—as in sit down and play with them and brush them a bit every day. If you can do this, you'll have less hair around the house when it's shedding season and you can care for them better.

For breeds like the pup's you have to keep a close eye on matting behind the ears, because it can get so out of control. Once that happens you pretty much have to cut the hair away because there's no combing it.

15. Eardrops, toothbrush/toothpaste, fish oil, glucosamine

Check with your vet on this kind of stuff. I have all of these now, but I didn't have them at the start. Pup hates the eardrops and I only manage them every other week or so. I think I've managed to brush her teeth about five times total. She does get the fish oil and glucosamine with her lunch after almost pulling her ACL a few months ago. But for each breed there will probably be things that help promote good health. Know what those are and when you should start using them.

16. No-Chew Spray

I can't believe I almost forgot this one. They have this bitter apple spray that you can buy and spray on surfaces to encourage a dog to stop chewing on it. This was invaluable to me.

Now, some breeds, including Newfies, like the taste of the spray, so you have to monitor the pup to see if it's effective. But I used this on my wooden tray tables, the carpet, the wall, the couch, the bed post, and the rear seat belts. It worked each time. (Although she would spend a lot of time licking it off of each surface, she didn't chew on them anymore and that's what counted.)

17. Towels For the Pup

Pups can't come inside and take off their shoes like humans do. Or change into dry clothes. When it snows or rains, you have a wet and dirty puppy. Best to keep a towel by the door to wipe them down a bit or you'll be spending a lot more time cleaning than you'd like.

ESTABLISH A ROUTINE

Like I said before, pups are adaptable. They'll adjust to whatever situation you put them in. But they do come to form certain expectations, so if you baby them too much too early you can run into issues later on.

When I first had the pup, I worked from home. And I was able to run to the store while she was sleeping, which meant she was rarely if ever alone. Well…that created some challenges. Because I eventually hit a point where I wanted to leave her alone for an hour or two to meet a friend for lunch, for example.

The first few times I did it were very traumatic for her. She'd never really been alone before.

After a bit I started deliberately leaving her alone a couple hours here or there just to get her used to the experience.

You should also try to establish a routine time for feeding and sleeping. This is harder in an apartment. I had an upstairs neighbor who got up at 4:30 every morning. Woke the pup up every single time. I'm still dealing with that to this day, because the pup still wakes up like clockwork at 4:38 each morning. Fortunately, she's learned to go back to sleep after a quick trip outside, but it still sucks.

My theory on this is to start how you want to finish it. I knew a woman that had never really left her dog alone for the first five years. After all that time when she did try taking it in to daycare, the dog had a complete meltdown.

Me? Daycare was my way to get a break without leaving the pup alone too long and her way to play with other dogs in a small, controlled environment. I used to take her in for about four hours at a pop once or twice a week.

Certainly came in handy when we moved and I had to work in an office for six months and she had to spend ten hours a day, five days a week at daycare

Whatever you think you'll need, get the pup used to it as early as you can.

THE GO BAG

After a few weeks of constantly forgetting something or other when I walked the pup, I put together a go bag. This is easier to pull off as a woman than a man, but I think it's pretty darned useful for anyone that lives in an apartment and has to walk their dog too many times a day.

I used a small, flat purse with multiple pockets that could fit over my shoulder and sit on my hip. The bag sat by the door and the minute pup signaled that we needed to go outside, I'd grab the bag and we'd be on our way. So, what was inside?

1. Poop Bags

You need the bags with you before your pup does its thing. If you get these for free where you live, grab extras and put them in the bag.

You are not going to have your puppy poop ten feet from the stand, wrestle the puppy over there to get a bag, and then go back to pick up after them. Not consistently. So be prepared.

And always have far more of these than you think you'll need. I had the pup use four or five on a single walk when she was feeling sick. Which was not always evident until we were already outside. She'd stop, get a little sick, I'd pick it up, she'd walk five feet, get a little sick, etc.

(As a side note—pick it up if your pup pukes outside. Otherwise someone else's dog will end up eating your dog's puke. Disgusting, yes, but that's what happens. Been there, seen it with my own eyes. Gives a whole new meaning to puppy kisses.)

Also, know that sometimes those free dispensers will be empty because the maintenance guy hasn't bothered to refill it. So be prepared. I had a roll of a hundred poop bags that I bought and carried in the bottom of my bag at all times just in case. (And I always had a few bags in every coat I owned, because I never knew when pup might decide she needed to do something and I didn't have the go bag with me.)

2. Flashlight

This one seems odd until you walk your pup at midnight and she decides to poop in that one spot that's dark as can be because it's midway between the street lights. You want to pick up after her, but you can't see your hand let alone what she just left on the grass. A flashlight solves that issue.

It also lets you see what your pup has taken such a sudden interest in, although you may wish you hadn't. And it lets you avoid all the poop that less considerate owners have left behind on the grass or sidewalk.

3. Treats

It may just be the breed, but Newfies are stubborn. When the pup was young she'd sometimes not want to come in. So she'd just plop her little butt down and refuse to move. When she weighed twenty pounds, I could just pick her up and take her in. She'd squirm and fight, but I won.

When she got closer to fifty pounds that was no longer an option. But treats? Oh, those worked like a charm. (So did asking her if she wanted to run and then running with her in the direction of the apartment.)

They also helped when she'd get fixated on something like a rabbit or other dog or person. I could hold the treat under her nose and suddenly she'd be far more interested in the treat than whatever had distracted her.

(I could also use the "look at me" command and she'd whirl around and stare at me, waiting for her treat instead of noticing whatever it was I didn't want her to see.)

(I also think this is probably why bigger dogs tend to be better behaved than smaller dogs. Because owners of big dogs have no choice. They can't just pick up their misbehaving dog like small dog owners can.)

4. Tissues or wet wipes

I don't even want to think about some of the things I've pulled out of the pup's mouth. It helps to have something to wipe your fingers with immediately after that happens.

Also, sometimes I'd get a runny nose and pup would have no interest in going inside. Having a pack of tissues handy helped tremendously.

5. Keys

Better than trying to find them when the pup needs outside right this minute. Just keep them with the go bag and there's no need to search for them—time during which the pup may just pee on the carpet.

6. Sunglasses

Not top priority when you're rushing your puppy outside, but a necessity if you're going to be outside for any length of time and it's daytime.

7. Gloves

Same as above. Easy to forget, but in much demand a few minutes after you're outside and have no way of going back for them.

WHAT TO TAKE TO THE PARK

I took the go bag almost everywhere. But there are additional items I would take for either the park or the dog park. This section is about going to the park.

When your pup is new you're not supposed to take them around other dogs. Their little puppy immune system can't handle the stresses. So, I would take my pup to a regular park and let her run around there. I had one near my house with five soccer fields and during the week during the day it was generally empty, so I could let her run a bit.

I'd also meet my mom for lunch sometimes at a park that had a little gazebo and the pup would hang out while we ate.

Here's what I took with me:

1. The go bag

Because all of that stuff still comes into play at the park. Especially the poop bags. You should always clean up after your dog. Always.

2. Water

I never took water if pup and I were just walking around the complex. (Although a few times when she wanted a marathon walk, I thought about how nice it would've been to have with me.) But I always took water to the park.

There are plenty of options out there for carrying a pup's water. My friend gave me one that had a built in water bowl which I really liked. My mom gave me one that was one unit that detached into pieces so she had a food bowl and water bowl in addition to the water holder.

Or you just bring a water bottle and the pup's water bowl from home. But if you're out and about enough, you'll want something you can just grab and go without thinking about it.

3. Toys

Puppies will eat anything. Every minute they have a toy in their mouth they don't have a piece of glass, a rock, a cigarette, a pine cone, geese poop, etc. in their mouth.

4. Blanket

Pup was pretty well-trained to know which blankets were hers, so I'd bring one of her blankets with us so she knew where I wanted her to lay down. It would take a while sometimes because she was busy exploring, but eventually she'd come back to her blanket. Nice thing with a blanket is that you know in that little space of cloth there's nothing else there that she can eat or get into.

5. Phone

I didn't generally take my phone with me when we walked around the complex. But I always had it with me when we drove anywhere. You never know what will happen. Always good to be able to phone a friend.

6. Wallet

Obvious, but easy to forget with puppy brain.

7. First Aid Kit

I never actually carried one. I think I now have one in my car because of a cross-country trip, but this could be very useful. What do you do if your pup cuts its foot on a piece of glass? Or gets in a fight with a cat? Or is attacked by another dog? (All of which have happened to someone's dog at some point.)

8. Tether

I didn't use this often, but my mom bought me one of those stakes you put in the ground that you can then tether a dog to so they can run around in a twenty-foot circle or whatever. Pup tended to try to outrun the tether and choke herself on it, so I settled for keeping her on her six-foot leash instead. She was more familiar with the limits of that and didn't have the same issues.

LETTING YOUR DOG LOOSE

Since I brought it up above, let's touch on letting your puppy loose. I have definitely done this.

One, I used to do this when the pup would play with other dogs. Otherwise you end up in the dance of leashes where the dogs are jumping and playing with one another and the owners are trying to dance around one another to keep everyone from getting tangled. It's a mess.

If I knew the pup was playing with one of her friends and wouldn't run away, I'd either drop her leash or take it off.

Now. This is not always a smart thing to do. We had a great central courtyard area at my first apartment and the pup had a friend she'd play with there. They'd always stay within the confines of the sidewalk, so it was fine. Until the day the pup's friend took off for the parking lot and pup followed right along behind.

We were fortunate. It was mid-day and there was no one around to hit them and they both eventually came back, but that could've been very, very bad.

Also, if you let your dog loose, they're no longer in your control. If they run off after a squirrel or rabbit or whatever, you can lose them. I once had the pup run across two soccer fields to go say hi to another dog.

(Although I learned another valuable lesson from that: As long as I was following, the pup felt comfortable continuing. If I could've brought myself to stay still or even walk the other direction, she very likely would've stopped and come back to me. I now use that trick at the dog park. Her limit is usually about fifty feet before she stops and turns back.)

WHAT TO TAKE TO THE DOG PARK

I take the pup to the dog park most days now even though we're in a house. (She's spoiled.) The dog parks we go to have water, so I don't generally bring water with us. Also, one has a lake she drinks out of. (I do, however, keep a water bowl in the car most of the time, so she's not completely deprived even if there's no water at the park.)

My list of what to bring to the dog park is more limited.

1. Go bag
2. Wallet
3. Keys
4. Phone
5. Park pass (if applicable)

At the dog park, your pup is going to be running around with other dogs, so no need for a blanket. And I'd leave anything you can't carry on you in the car.

I don't tend to bring toys. Where we go, there are always extra tennis balls lying around. And pup has never managed to keep the same ball from start to finish, especially when a body of water is involved. In DC, we went to a dog park with a river in it and she'd take her tennis balls out to the middle of the river and drop them there. In the park with a lake, she'll swim out to grab a ball and then drop it the minute her feet touch the bottom of the lake, which is generally about three or four feet from shore.

I occasionally do contribute a few tennis balls to the park, but generally I just pick up the ones we find there.

Some people bring fancy toys with them and then get very cranky if any other dog takes the toy or tries to play with their dog. It's a dog park. Dogs will play with each other and take each others' toys. If you want a private play session with expensive toys, find somewhere private or you'll be very disappointed.

DOG PARK ETIQUETTE

Chances are if you have a dog in an apartment you will find yourself at the dog park or in the dog run next to the apartment building. Your dog needs to run.

So, how to behave?

1. Pick up after your dog.

Dog parks and dog runs are not places where you get to take your dog so it can poop and you can ignore it. Sorry. You chose to have a dog in an apartment which means you also signed up for the privilege of picking up its crap for the time being.

This also means keeping your dog in sight so you can see when your dog craps. Many dog owners are social. That's great. But no one likes the dog owner who's busy blabbing to their new-found friends while Fido is over in the corner taking a crap. People notice even if no one says anything.

2. Control your dog

Pup is now close to a hundred pounds. She's not mean with other dogs, but she's big. So if she wants to play with a smaller breed of dog I keep a very close eye on her and the minute it looks like that dog is upset, scared, or (more likely) its owner is upset, I pull her away. I know she won't hurt the other dog, but that doesn't matter. Every dog should be able to enjoy itself at the park.

The place I take the pup there's a guy who has no control over his dogs and one of them harasses the pup every time it sees her. Now, when someone's dog seeks shelter between their legs or behind them, that means the dog is scared. If your dog is the reason, grab them and pull them away. Put them on leash and lead them elsewhere.

Better yet, anticipate the situation and lead your dog away before it ever happens.

3. Be friendly

Say hi. You don't have to exchange names and numbers, but be nice to the people and dogs that are there. It makes everyone's experience better. It's as simple as a quick smile and nod to anyone you pass or who walks by.

4. Keep your dog leashed in the parking lot area

I can't tell you how many times I closed my eyes and turned away because someone let their dog run through the parking lot ahead of them and a car almost hit the dog. Your dog may not be the type to run away, but if someone doesn't see it, they may hit it. Not fun. So, leash your dog up.

It's also considerate of other owners that are trying to control their own dogs and either get them into the car or out of it.

5. Think long and hard before you bring your children with you

I've seen a five-year-old girl knocked down by a wrestling group of dogs. And, you know what? It was the parents' fault. They brought the girl and then didn't control her at all and she ran out into the middle of the dog's play area. It's a dog park, it's for dogs.

If you do bring kids, instruct them how to behave. That same lovely family also had a little boy running around screaming at the dogs calling them bad dogs for playing. Excuse me? That's why the dogs were there.

Even well-behaved kids can be in danger at a dog park. Dogs play rough. They tackle each other and run around and anyone who gets in their way can be knocked down, including full-grown adults. So think long and hard before exposing your child to that.

6. Ask before giving treats to other dogs

If you can avoid it, you should probably not even bring treats. I do because it's how I get the pup to leave without a fuss. If you do bring treats, expect other dogs to come running the minute they smell them or hear the bag.

First, try to only treat your dog when other dogs aren't around. But if they do come running, look to the owner and ask, "Is it okay if I give your dog a treat?" Some dogs have allergies and others just aren't good at taking treats. You don't want to get bit or be the reason someone's dog gets sick.

7. Teach your dog not to jump

I've seen this multiple times. There's a dog park regular whose dog loves to jump on people. Now, I wear sweats and ratty clothes to the dog park because I have no real expectation of leaving there clean. Still. That doesn't mean I signed up for a sixty-pound dog to jump on me.

Each time I've seen this the owner was very apologetic, but I saw those dogs for months at a time and the owners never broke them of the habit. If you can't get your dog to stop jumping, put them on a leash until they do. Or don't bring them.

(And on the jumping issue, understand that something that seems cute or harmless when you're pup is fifteen pounds will not be when it's full-grown. Don't let behavior that's going to be problematic slide just because the pup is small and cute.)

8. If your dog takes another dog's toy, offer to give it back

Like I said, I just find tennis balls at the park for the pup to use. If other dogs show up and they want to chase a ball with her, I have no problem with it even if they run away with the ball.

But I've had the pup take another dog's ball. When that happens, I always ask if they want it back. And, if they do, I bribe her into giving it back. I view most toys as communal, but not everyone does. And even for those who do, if your dog found a toy and is happily playing with it, sometimes you don't want to lose it. So ask.

9. Don't smoke. If you do, take your butts with you

I can't honestly remember ever seeing anyone smoking at a dog park. But I have seen cigarette butts. Since pup tried to eat those when she was young, I am never happy to see them. If you must smoke, don't leave the butts on the ground for some dog to eat.

EXERCISING YOUR DOG

I kind of touched on it above, but I'll say it again: Your dog needs exercise. Walks every day, certainly. Depending on size and breed, how much and how far will vary greatly, but something.

And I fully believe that every dog needs the opportunity to run around. A small breed dog may have enough space to do so in an apartment. A big breed dog will need to go elsewhere.

Even at twenty pounds my pup needed somewhere to stretch her legs. Otherwise she ran these insane circles around the apartment where I swore she was going to hurt herself any minute.

When she was little I'd take her to the park and let her run around on the soccer fields.

When she was older we'd go to dog parks.

When I was in DC and I couldn't get her to the dog park, I'd take her to a dog run at a nearby building.

If she didn't get enough exercise she was a pain in the ass. She wanted to go outside over and over again, or would cry or chew things or…

My life and hers were much easier on the days she got to stretch her legs.

Now, having said that, if you have a larger breed dog, don't overdo it. Until your dog is finished growing, you need to watch how much you stress its bones and joints. For Newfies, you're not supposed to exercise them more than they'd get running around in the yard for the first two years. So no ten-mile hikes or long runs. Know your breed and exercise it accordingly.

TOYS – GENERAL

I mentioned it above, but your pup will need toys. I tried to give the pup toys of different textures. She had Nylabones and stuffed animals and Kongs and things that crinkled and things that squeaked and things that made other weird noises.

Depending on the day, she might play with all of them. Or just one.

The key with toys is that you have to monitor your puppy's behavior with their toy. Even now I have to. I don't sit over her like a hawk or anything, but a puppy can be great with a toy for days or weeks on end and then suddenly decide to destroy it.

Pup had a hedgehog she loved. It was big and stuffed and she'd sleep on it all the time. Well, about six weeks after I brought her home, I noticed all these black strings in her poop. Turned out she'd developed a fascination with pulling the hair out of her toys. The poor hedgehog was bald. A few weeks later, our trainer gave her a toy with hair and she immediately started pulling all its hair out.

After weeks of not having an issue, I had to either deny her toys with hair or modify them to remove the hair. I "beheaded" one of her multi-squeaker toys. (Things you can do with dog's toys that you'd never do with kid's toys.)

I also knew that, as much as she loved rope toys, I couldn't leave her alone with them. She'd start pulling out the threads and then I'd hear this little hacking noise and reach into her mouth and pull out a mass of strings she'd taken off it. We could play with a toy like that together and it would be fine, but she could never play with them alone.

Each dog is different. You'll have to watch and learn what they can and can't have. My brother's dogs destroy all toys. Pup has about twenty that she's generally fine with. Until, of course, the day she isn't…

PULLING CRAP OUT OF YOUR PUP'S MOUTH

This is probably a good time to talk about pulling things out of your pup's mouth. Without a doubt, your pup will eat or swallow something it should not. With the pup, she tore apart a pillow she originally slept on and I found a huge wad of stuffing in the back of her throat. Another time I pulled a six-inch string out of her mouth.

And that's not counting the pinecones, rabbit poop, leaves, dead animals, etc. that I removed at various points in time.

Now, this could be her breed, but she's generally pretty good at letting me do that. Why? Well, I started that way on day one. The first time she grabbed something she shouldn't, I opened her jaws and fished it back out. And I did that every single time I saw it happen.

She once somehow found a dead crawfish. That one I didn't touch. But I did pry her jaws open and direct her mouth at the ground so she dropped it.

Nice thing is, after about ten days of that, whatever it was that she liked to eat, she stopped eating. So, leaves, pine cones, etc. she doesn't eat when I'm around. (She developed a habit of eating sticks from an outdoor daycare she went to for a bit.

And of swallowing the pieces, too. Which made for a pleasant puking experience one night. That one I've never really managed to break her of.)

If you can fish things out of your dog's mouth, I think it helps. If not, then don't. But remember, you're supposed to be the alpha to your dog. They may not like it, but they should let you do it. (Check your breed, of course. Like I said, Newfs are known to be pretty mellow dogs.)

BACK TO TOYS – THE NOISE ISSUE

One of the problems with having a dog in an apartment is the noise they make. Barking is the main issue, but noisy toys are, too.

When I first had the pup, she slept in my room. And I'd bring in a few toys for her to play with because she'd sometimes wake up in the middle of the night or need a little time to wind-down before she fell asleep. Well, problem was most of her toys were noisy.

Rubber toys? Squeaky as hell.

Squeaker toys? Also squeaky. And I don't think I ever found a stuffed animal toy for dogs that didn't have a squeaker somewhere. Once the pup discovered the squeaker in a new toy I had to banish it to the front room.

Again, in a house, who cares? But in an apartment, you have to think about the neighbors.

PUKE AND POOP

I've alluded to it before, but if you have a puppy, it will puke and it will have diarrhea. It just will.

If you're in a house, you might not even notice. The dog will run outside, puke, eat it back up, and you'll be none the wiser.

In an apartment? You'll see it or hear it happening.

Pup had this period of time where she was eating too fast. She'd scarf her food down and then five minutes later puke it all back up. (Solution: Feed her smaller amounts over a longer period of time and/or wet and heat her food so it was mushy.) We also had the stick-eating incident where she ate a stick and then puked it all back up in the middle of the night.

You will see and handle puppy puke. Be prepared.

Also, chances are your pup will have some loose stools. Its food might not agree with it, it might eat something it shouldn't, it might pick up giardia, it might get stressed. Pup has been sick to her stomach for all of the above reasons.

Never fun. And, again, something you may not have to deal with in a house, but will definitely have to deal with in an apartment. When pup had giardia, we were up two or three times a night for her to go outside.

THE FIGHTS YOU LOSE

I swore pup would never sleep on the couch and she'd never drink out of the toilet.

I lost both fights.

Because, to win those fights, you have to be consistent about it every single time. And I wasn't. She was pretty damned cute when she first started trying to sleep on the couch. She'd get half up so her back legs were still on the ground and try to sleep that way. Or she'd fall so sound asleep on the couch that she'd roll herself right off. It was adorable.

Now she generally sleeps on her beds, but she'll still get up on the couch at times. I just decided I'd let it happen.

She also has her own toilet she gets to drink out of. I avoided that one until DC when we ended up with two bathrooms. I figured no one was using the second one, so what the hell.

Assume that whatever you thought the rules would be, that you'll cave on some of them.

BUT. Be sure that anything you don't want the dog to do full-grown, you don't let them do as a puppy. Like jumping up. Or riding in your lap in the car. Pick your battles and be sure you win them every time.

RIDING IN THE CAR

The best advice one of my friends gave me was that I get the pup used to riding in the car as soon as possible. When the pup and I then had to move from Colorado to DC and spent six to eight hours a day driving cross-country, I blessed that man for his sage advice.

Get your dog used to the car. You will take the dog to the vet. You may want to just drive the dog around to get away from the apartment. If you go to the dog park, that will probably require a car ride, too. And, if you move, you'll need to drive the pup to the new home.

Some do's and don't's:

1. Do create a space for the dog where it can sit without interfering with your driving

When we brought the pup home, she was so scared, she rode in my lap, shaking like a leaf the whole time. She could stand on my thighs and rest her chin on my arm back then. Now? Oh holy cow! I'd be screwed if she tried to do that.

About three weeks after I got her, I started making her ride in the back.

I think we've established that I give her a lot of preference. I have the luxury of doing this, because I don't have kids or other dogs and I rarely have anyone else ride in my car. So, what I did was put the back seats up so they blocked her access to the front of the car and gave her run of the back. She has more space in the car than I do.

Key, though, is she doesn't have the ability to interfere with me while I'm driving.

She can and does stand on the armrest in the back and put her head on my shoulder, but that's about it. (She once puked down my back doing that—fun times.)

Some people put crates in their car or have screens or even doggie seat belts. Do whatever works for you, but start as early as possible with getting the pup into a manageable space.

2. Don't let your dog hang its head out the window.

I know, they love it. Problem is, they can hurt themselves if they get something in their eyes or noses. Crack the window so they have some fresh air, but not enough for them to put their face outside the car.

Also, be sure to use the kiddie lock function on your windows. My mom had a scary incident where one of her dogs hit the window button and rolled the window up on itself, choking itself. The dog was panicked and it was very hard for her to get it free. I've had the pup roll the window down on me when I forgot to lock it and then had to worry she was going to try to jump out of the car before I could fix it.

3. Do make sure that water is available if you're on the road for any length of time.

After much experimentation and a very wet floor mat, I now have a no-spill bowl that I use in the car for the pup. When I pick her up from daycare, she generally guzzles water. And when we were traveling cross-country she needed that available because we only stopped every couple hours. (I placed it behind the passenger's seat so I could easily reach and refill it if needed.)

4. Do think about adding padding or a bed

When the seats are removed in the back of my vehicle, there are gaps where the seats fit into the floor and there's also a bolt that sticks up from the floor. Putting a bed or padding over those helps protect the pup from injury.

5. Do provide toys or distractions on long trips

Pup travels like a champ. She will stand at my shoulder and just watch the world go by. But she eventually gets bored. And when she does, if she doesn't have a toy or something to occupy her, one of two things happens. She starts crying. (Always fun while stuck in rush hour traffic on the highway.) Or she starts chewing something.

On the way to DC, she managed to chew almost all the way through the rear seat belt and chew part of her bed before I realized that I had to give her toys and bones to distract her.

6. Don't set the temperature to what you want

Dogs have a different way of keeping cool than we do. I find with my pup that I have to always keep the temperature a little cooler than I'd prefer in order to keep her comfortable. This is especially true in wintertime.

I can see with some breeds where the exact opposite could be true. So, set the temp to something the pup can manage. You do not want to give your pup heatstroke.

7. Don't leave your pup alone in the car.

Now, having said that, I have. It was just the pup and I driving cross-country to and from DC. Eight hours of driving a day, I had to pee sometimes. That was really hard when we drove back from DC in July. Temperatures were in the high 90's on that trip and if I'd left the pup in the car for any length of time, she'd have died. Or ended up with heatstroke, which would've been very, very bad.

So, if you must leave your dog in the car, do it for as short a time as you can manage. When I was traveling, I'd run into a fast food place, order, use the bathroom, grab my order, and get back to her. It generally took less than five minutes.

I also made sure to crack all the windows so she was cooler than if I'd left the windows up and the heat had been baking into her.

Cold temperatures are an issue as well. If it's freezing out, the dog can freeze to death. May take longer than heat stroke, but it can happen. So, minimize the time if you can.

COMMANDS YOU SHOULD KNOW

This is just general puppy parenting here.

One of the best things I did (even though pup seldom listens to me on the whole drop it/leave it thing without a treat these days), is take the pup to obedience classes. They taught us how to walk our dogs, how to get them to sit and come, how to get them to drop things or leave things be. It was great. It was a lifesaver.

So, here are the commands I learned and when I used them:

1. Look At Me

It's a command that has the pup stare at you. Very handy when walking the pup and I needed her to look away from something else. She'd immediately sit and stare at my face. I used it all the time after we learned it.

2. Sit

Also handy. Generally in a store or other situation where you need the pup to stay in place.

3. Leave It

A good command for getting a dog to ignore something they want to eat. (Sometimes needs to be combined with drop it. As in, drop it, now leave it.)

This one actually helped break the pup of a biting thing she developed. When she needed to poop she'd jump on the couch and start biting me. Very painful. I was at my wit's end trying to break her of the habit. Until I did a little googling and found out that leave it can be used to get a puppy to stop any sort of action you don't want.

Worked like a charm. She doesn't bite anymore and I love her far more because of that.

4. Drop It

Excellent command for when you're too late to tell the pup to leave it. As noted above, sometimes has to be followed by leave it. Otherwise, the pup will drop the thing, count to two, and pick it right back up.

5. Stay

Good for, well, getting a puppy to stay in place.

6. Come

This one is so obvious, I forgot to include it the first time I wrote this. Walking around the apartment complex you probably won't need this, but if you go to a dog park or let your dog off leash, it definitely comes in handy. They say to use a special treat that you only use for this command to ensure that the dog listens, but I never managed that myself.

We learned other commands that I don't really use. Like heel and go to your bed. Both can be incredibly useful, but I'm just not that formal with my dog. If I need her to walk next to me, I have a knot tied in her six-foot leash that lets me bring her right by my side. It doesn't require a command, she just does it.

And I never send her to her bed. She's rarely if ever in my way. (One thing to keep in mind with these commands. If you don't use them, you will lose them. So, if you think you'll need one in the future, be sure to use it enough with the pup so it's available when you do need it.)

FEEDING YOUR DOG HUMAN FOOD

I don't know if this works with every dog, but when I got the pup I decided not to feed her human food. I'm not sure why, I've fed every dog I've ever had cheese or carrots or bits of meat, but with her I decided I wouldn't.

And one of the amazing, wonderful results of that choice is that she has no interest in my food. I can leave a plate with bacon on it in the living room and she'll ignore it.

Now, we've run into a few issues over time as I've had to give her human food for various reasons. I gave her tons of carrots when she was teething. And pumpkin when she had a sick stomach. And chicken and rice, also for a sick stomach. So, she's wised up a bit, but she'd still rather have a rawhide than my steak.

It makes meals that much more pleasant.

WHAT TO DO FOR A SICK STOMACH

My pup had lots of stomach issues. Not sure if it was a bit of allergies. A few times it was giardia. Sometimes it was just randomness. What I found that worked.

1. Tylan Powder

This is a miracle drug. I don't have it anymore and most vets don't even use it, I don't think, but there was a point where pup got sick almost every time I took her to the dog park. A sixteenth of a teaspoon of tylan powder and she was back to normal. Do not ask me how it worked, but it did.

2. Pumpkin

For a while there I had the pup on two tablespoons of pumpkin a day. It's great for a pup with stomach issues. Either constipation or diarrhea. It just helps even them out.

3. Chicken and sticky rice

You overcook white rice and boil chicken and feed that to the pup for about a day instead of their normal food. Also works fantastically.

Sometimes none of that will work because the pup has something like giardia. But I reached a point with my vet where they told me to try these things before I bothered bringing her in to see them.

A GREAT VET IS WORTH THEIR WEIGHT IN GOLD

The first six or seven months, the pup and I were at the vet all the frickin' time.

She had a sinus infection when I got her. (Long green snot coming out of a dog's nose? Not normal.)

Then she got an eye infection. (Try giving a smart dog eye drops twice a day for ten days. You will run out of ways to trick her long before the ten days are up.)

Then she got giardia.

Then her anal glands needed emptying

Then I panicked and thought she'd broken a tooth when her first back tooth fell out. (It doesn't look all cute and small and intact like the front ones do. It's flat and bloody. Don't panic.)

Then she got giardia again.

Then she had random stomach issues.

Then we tried to spay her and she failed the blood test.

Then we spayed her.

Then she got a urinary tract infection.

Then…

Yeah. We were at the vet a lot.

When I was in Colorado I had the vet of all vets. He was amazing with her. He'd get down on the floor and play with her and make her comfortable before he started the exam. (Still does.) Great prices. He didn't even charge me for the tooth incident. They were almost always able to get the pup in same day when needed. Big exam rooms. Hardly ever made me wait.

When we moved to DC I had no idea who to go to, so we went to Banfield. Overpriced. Small rooms. Most of the vets had no bedside manner. Took the pup's temperature (up the ass) every single time we were there no matter the reason. Ordered every test under the sun every single time. Made me wait over an hour on more than one occasion.

They were awful and ridiculous. Only good thing about them was that they were open seven days a week.

So, shop around, ask around, but find a good vet. They're out there.

(And, what I found worked best for getting the pup to take pills? Peanut butter. Cheese, she ate and spit the pill back out. Same with pill pockets. But peanut butter? Worked like a charm. Otherwise you're stuck putting the pill in the back of the pup's throat and triggering their gag reflex. Not fun for the pup or you.)

MAKE FRIENDS WITH YOUR NEIGHBORS AND MANAGEMENT

What else should you know?

Make friends with the management of your apartment building. When I was in DC it was far more challenging because I had to take the pup on elevators and through the lobby multiple times a day and, as I mentioned, there were a lot of anti-dog people in the building.

What saved me was the fact that the front desk staff loved the pup. They'd give her too many treats, but that was okay. Because they loved her. And on the rare occasions I had issues with someone else, they knew that she was generally a great dog and it was just a minor incident.

If they hadn't known her? We may have been kicked out. All they had to do was invoke the weight limit written into the contract that they'd verbally agreed to waive.

Same with your neighbors. If they like the pup, they'll be more forgiving of the occasional barking incident. You need them on your side, so make friends.

DEALING WITH CHILDREN

One last thought. When you have a puppy, one of the biggest challenges can be dealing with kids.

Kids obviously love puppies, but many are not knowledgeable about how to approach them and they will cause you all sorts of issues because some also don't listen well.

I remember one girl rode a scooter right up to the pup, fast, and made her so scared she peed herself. Then the girl tried to rename the pup because she didn't like the pup's name. She also held her hand right above the pup's nose and kept jerking it away. (A good way to get bit by a less mellow dog.)

Oh, and she got down on all fours and crawled around barking at the pup once, too.

Another kid would follow us around not talking or anything, just hovering about two feet behind us. If I stopped he'd then walk up and start petting the pup without asking or talking or anything.

And then there was the girl who insisted that her dog wanted to meet the pup even though her dog was cowering behind the girl's legs and clearly hadn't wanted anything to do with the pup.

Kids also tend to be loud and scream and make sudden movements, which can cause your pup to bark or get scared.

That can also then lead to the kids getting scared, which can then lead to the parents getting angry.

And, guess what? It's always your fault. Never the kid's. So, be prepared.

Kids are great, I love them. But around puppies, they can be a real challenge to deal with.

(I kept the kids away from the pup for about a month by telling them she still had giardia and could be contagious…Worked great. And, no, I don't regret it at all. You scare my puppy so bad she pees herself you have no business near her.)

CONCLUSION

So there you have it. I hope this helped.

Parenting a puppy is a big responsibility.

At least, if you care about the puppy and want it to have a good life it is. Anyone can lock a pup in a crate ten hours a day and yell at it when it cries as they sit on the couch eating ice cream and watching reality TV. I assume since you read this, that you're not that type of person.

I gave up a lot when I took on the pup. (I'd probably be living in New Zealand right now if I hadn't taken her on. I'd also be sleeping in past five each morning.)

But it's been more than worth it. She is an amazing little creature. She keeps me active. She makes me more caring and considerate. She makes me more social. She helps me see what my real priorities in life are.

It's been a life-changing experience, but worth every moment. I wish you the best of luck with it.

Just remember with dogs that the more you give them, the more you'll get back from them. They are intensely loyal creatures, but they also remember every little slight or hurt you give them.

So when they tear up one of your expensive shoes or pee on the carpet, which will happen, take a deep breath and address them calmly. Give them love and remember they don't know what you want until you show them. Praise good behavior, ignore bad.

(For accidents, the best thing is to ignore the accident and take the pup outside immediately if you see it happen. Otherwise, just clean it up and make sure to take the pup out every single time after it eats or wakes up from a nap. And then praise the holy hell out of your dog when it pees outside. It'll learn peeing outside means praise, peeing inside gets it nothing. Supposedly, small dogs that get yelled at will actually take to peeing in strange corners or places where you won't find it. They don't stop peeing inside, they just find ways not to be yelled at. So, praise, not shouts.)

Anyway. Best of luck! And many years of happiness with your little bundle of joy.

ABOUT THE AUTHOR

Cassie Leigh is the proud puppy parent of an adorable and incorrigible Newfoundland named Miss Priss. (I know. That name…)

She has lots of opinions and a few useful suggestions about surviving those first months of parenting a puppy in an apartment. It's not necessarily easy, but it is definitely worth it.

You can reach her at cassieleighauthor@gmail.com

www.ingramcontent.com/pod-product-compliance
Lightning Source LLC
Chambersburg PA
CBHW052203110526
44591CB00012B/2059